THE

WOLF SPIRIT

THE

WOLF SPIRIT

WAYS TO SHARE LIFE WITH YOUR DOG

by Barrie Tierney

illustrated by Jennifer Holt

WINGS
PUBLISHERS

Published by
WINGS PUBLISHERS
3555 Knollwood Drive
Atlanta, Georgia 30305

Text © 1999 by Barrie Tierney
Illustrations © 1999 Jennifer Holt

Book design by Melanie M. McMahon

Manufactured in the United States of America

10 9 8 7 6 5 4 3 2 1
First Edition

ISBN 0-9668884-5-6

DEDICATION

As with all things…
this is for Sara, Devin, Jillian, and the dogs.

Contents

FOREWORD

I have much to share with you. Beautiful stories of canine devotion, humorous stories of canine cleverness, inspiring stories of courage and strength. But first I have an obligation to fulfill. First, I must share with you the knowledge it takes to decide whether or not you want a dog, whether or not you should have a dog, and then, having decided to have one, how to choose the right dog and then what to do with the dog once you have it.

Please be aware of the fact that relating with a dog is a spiritual work. It isn't a matter of formulas, gizmos equipment, schedules and the like, although these things have their place. As with every great conductor, musician, artist, philosopher or healer, their success was a matter of inspiration, not law or math.

We humans are number one on planet earth, dogs are a close second. There was a time when this rating was reversed. The humans followed the wolf, learned from him and surpassed him. But nowhere in nature does the bright and creative sharing of life, love, work exist as it does between dog and man. This sharing is a spiritual thing; it exists because of the spiritual essence of the wolf and man-we are kin. So let's celebrate wolf spirit, let's love our dog and let's emulate the wolf in our attempt to share life with him.

A note to the reader: Throughout this book, I refer to dogs in both the male and female form. The Wolf Spirit methods apply equally and as effectively to both genders.

ABOUT DOGS AND MEN

Hello, my name is Barrie Tierney, although a great many dogs and people know me as their "Wicked Uncle Barrie." You can decide whether or not that's true as you read. To begin with I would like you to, at least for the time being, forget anything you may have heard or read about dog training, and I'll tell you why . . .

It happens on a regular basis—I'll get a call from a desperate person who has hired three trainers; two of whom were mauled, a third who ran away. The vet tells them that the dog must be put down. Now, at this point, you see,

> Before you do ANYTHING ELSE, you MUST establish the right relationship with your dog.

every conventional technique of dog training (and probably some not-so-conventional) has been tried on this dog—with no results. I go to this person's house and it takes me about five minutes to turn that dog around.

The reason that I can do this successfully is that I know how to establish the right relationship with the dog in those first five minutes—and that's what's been missing up to this point in the dog's life. And that's also what's generally missing in books on dog training. When you have finished reading this book, you, too, will know the secret of establishing the right relationship. Everything else has a way of falling into line once you've done that.

So what is that relationship? Well, it's probably very hard to see when you look at a bichon frise or a basset hound, but the correct relationship with your dog is one that duplicates wolf communication and the structure of the wolf pack. Now, before we go any further with this, I must give you some background on dogs and wolves and men.

There are about thirty or so canine animals that inhabit the planet earth. Of these 30-odd canines, there are half a dozen dogs. This group includes the wolf, the true domesticated dog, a couple of African jackals, the coyote, and the dingoes. The wolf and the coyote can mate with the domesticated dog to produce fertile offspring. It is possible that your dog has the bloodline of any of these dogs in his veins, but far and away (in most cases) he is closer to the wolf than any of the others. So we will celebrate the spirit of the wolf that is in him and look there for guidance on what to do.

The species *canis lupus,* as a completed species, the way we see him today, is far older than man. There was a time when the species we've come to call humans admired these guys in the gray suits who lived at a fixed address on the bank overlooking the river and ruled the area. As man became aware that the wolf was living better than we were, we began to imitate the wolf. We became a hunter-gatherer society. We followed along the same game trail, the same migratory patterns as the wolf. And, we competed with the wolf for his diet—the hunter-gatherer's diet—roots, nuts, berries, meat. Now I know there is a raging argument right now as to exactly when this happened. And, I would love to go into much greater detail on this. But what I am going to do here is encapsulate some of these things, just to give you an idea about how they apply to training your dog.

Although the things I'm about to tell you are abbreviated, for our purposes they are essentially accurate. Imagine early man admiring wolves. He sees how well they function together as a group—how well they work a herd of caribou, for example—and knows if he could have this animal as an ally, it would be a tremendous asset. But, of course, wolves, by and large, don't want to have anything to do with man and with good reason. But as early man learned how to selectively breed animals, there came a time when he bred the dog from the wolf.

I think it's quite possible that the wolf was the first animal that man experimented with when attempting selective breeding. After a few false starts, he probably figured out how the system worked. What he learned basically was this. If you take the smallest brother and sister from a litter of wolf cubs and breed them together, you're "in-breeding" the pair. Since in-breeding draws out recessive genetic traits, like smallness, this smallest brother and sister are going to produce pups that are abnormally small. Take the smallest brother and sister from that litter and breed them together and you accelerate the process. In a very short time you're going to go from 120 pounds of *canis lupus* to a 30-pound animal that now views wolves as something strange to be attacked or run from, while it views you as its close companion. You now have bred a true, domesticated dog. I think this is basically the route that early man took with the wolves.

Years pass, breeding continues, and modern man has now reached the place where he can breed 30 pounds of cocker spaniel or a 5-pound Yorkie . But I want you to realize that very little went into this true domesticated dog other than wolf. So your true domesticated dog, the animal we're concerned with here, is not only descended from wolves, but is a wolf in a different shape. And for this reason, in this training method, we duplicate wolf communication and we duplicate pack structure. That's where your dog's strongest urges are found; that's where he is most easily led. So, how do we duplicate wolf communication? That's the topic of the next chapter.

DUPLICATING WOLF COMMUNICATION AND PACK STRUCTURE

Wolves, being an ancient breed, have developed a workable plan for keeping order in the pack. Basically, to ensure their survival, wolves need each and every member of the pack to achieve success—in wolf terms, of course. You are going to ensure your dog's success in

> Everything we do with our dogs must be done out of love and respect and a desire for mutual success.

the training process by helping him follow the instincts of his wolf spirit and by assuming the "Alpha" role—becoming the leader of the pack—in your relationship with him. Let me tell you how and why this works.

Everything we do with our dog must be done out of love and respect and a desire for mutual success. That's what motivates a wolf pack; therefore, that's our motivation here. Not fear, not anger, not frustration. These are tiring, draining emotions. If love is our motivation, we are tireless. If we give love and respect and a desire for mutual success to our dog, our dog will give that right back to us. If we decide that our dog is a stupid flea bag, our dog will oblige us by being precisely that. So, love, respect, and a desire for mutual success are our only motivators.

There is another ingredient in this formula, and that's consistency. If a thing is right, it should always be right and never, ever wrong. If a thing is wrong it's always wrong and it's never, ever going to be right. Now there are some gray areas here. For example, my dogs know that they can never ever jump on me or put their paws on me. However, if I bend slightly forward at the waist, folding my arm out as if I were looking at my watch, my dogs know that I want paws on this arm. And now that I've begun this process, I can hug the dog, examine its belly for ticks, tweak him on the nose, whatever. But you see, even though there's a gray area, it is still clearly defined—the only time that he can jump on me is when I've made that one, specific gesture.

All right, now let's talk about the right and wrong things. I'm going to draw two scenarios for you and let you begin to see how all this works. You will see how we make sure that our best friend, our dog, knows what we want him to do (the right thing) and what we don't (the wrong) and how we get him to recognize the correct behaviors at his deepest level—that of instinct.

Let's say that you are standing in the back yard and your dog is hopping around out there, amusing himself, when he looks up and notices you. Well, he starts wagging his tail and trots on over to you. He nuzzles your leg, licks the back of your hand, then sits attentively as if to say "well, what are we going to do?" All right, this is what we had in mind when we got our dog, our beautiful friend—he's seen us, acknowledged us, trotted over to us—now we're sharing this beautiful affection and we're trying to decide what sort of wonderful adventure we're going to go on.

All of this is good. And even though we didn't ask the dog to do it, we are compelled to praise him. This is the very first step: every time you see your dog doing something good, praise the dog. There's no precise formula for praising. But, you should know this—the human body flows with an

PRAISE

electrical current. Different emotions and motivations cause this current to change. Your dog is a carnivore. He's got the equipment in his head to analyze that change. He can smell and he can feel when you are mad, confused, upset, happy, confident. So, when you relate with your dog, he's reading you at all times, and you can't fool him. So, knowing this, we feel the love, the respect, and the gratitude. Then, with our calm, quiet hand—mark this, hands are used in gentleness only because we want the dog to have supreme confidence in our hands—we gently praise the dog. "What a Good Boy!" Make it a firm, loving caress. There's nothing wrong with pulling the dog next to you, pulling him against your leg, and saying "What a Good Boy!" That's praising a dog—it's very simple.

But let's get to reality here. This is the second, and much more common scenario. If your dog's a puppy, chances are you step into your back yard, he sees you, starts wagging his tail, and comes charging across the yard. He leaves the ground about three feet from you, and "Kaboom!" smashes into you, a wiggling, barking, arching, mass of (canine) joy. This is unacceptable. Please don't let your dog jump on you. It might be cute when he's a puppy, but if he grows up to weigh 60 pounds and hits you at 30 miles an hour—let me tell you, it's not going to be cute! And besides, it can alarm people who aren't necessarily familiar with dogs. So now we have to correct this pup. And correction is a precise ritual. Again, we are going to correct him out of love and respect and a desire for mutual success. We will not be angry with our dog. We will correct him because we love him.

To find out the best way to do this, let's transport our dog to a wolf pack and assume that they've accepted him. Now, what would actually happen is that the first wolf that saw him would say "Oh, a snack, that's interesting!" But let's assume that they've accepted him, and let's assume that he's run across the clearing and smacked into the Alpha (wolf). That is an unacceptable act. You do not crash into the Alpha (and the Alpha is what you need to be in your dog's eyes).

Your dog views his relationship with you as a pack relationship. He's a member of your pack. And he *wants* you to be the leader. Dogs want leadership. Again, imagine your dog as a member of the wolf pack. He's crashed into the Alpha, and the Alpha (again, out of love and respect and a desire for his success) is going to begin a five-step correction. For our purposes, I'm going to break this correction pattern—this ritual that's older than man—into five steps that are very easily understood by both you and your dog.

STEP 1

In the Pack: At the moment of impact the Alpha is going to omit a sharp, short exhalation of breath—wolves don't bark, but they do emit sharp growls.

Human/Dog Translation: We're going to use the word "NO!" It works very well. And, we're going to say it just like a bark—short, sharp, clipped—"NO!" You can say it in a loud voice, you can say it with a stage whisper— either is equally effective.

STEP 2

In the Pack: The second thing the Alpha is going to do is pause for a fraction of a second.

Human/Dog Translation: This is what you will do, too. You allow a brief pause to give your dog a "cue" that he must obey or there will be a consequence.

STEP 3

In the Pack: Immediately following this pause, the Alpha wolf is going to bite this new pack member (your dog) on the neck or the side of the face. This bite is not to administer pain or damage, but it is a physical conse-quence, a warning. Remember, the Alpha is doing this out of love.

Human/Dog Translation: (Relax, I don't want you to bite your dog. It's a good way to get locked up! Or, bitten back!) What we're going to do is use a leash to duplicate the "bite." When training your dog, you must have the dog on leash. First, make sure that the leash is slack. To duplicate the wolf's technique, we're going to give that leash a sudden, sharp, tug—we'll call it a "snap."

It is important to remember that any time you have your dog with you on a leash that leash is to be slack. Anytime that your dog puts sudden or forceful pressure on that leash, you get the slack back with a snap. We'll discuss this more later. But now, the last two steps.

STEPS 4 AND 5

In the Pack: After the Alpha has bitten your dog, he's going to study him for five seconds or so, gauging his response; making sure that he's properly accepting this correction **(Step 4).**

When the Alpha's recorded that fact for about five seconds or so and determined he's gotten the response he's after, he's going to **(Step 5)** relax his posture and stare, releasing the tension of the moment. He then may give a reassuring little nuzzle, as if to say "go on, kid, get out of here!" This is how he proves his Alpha authority. It's as if he's saying: "Hey, it's all right, I'm not mad, I'm not upset. You did that—I did this. If you do that again, I'll do this again. And we'll keep going until you stop or you're left too crippled to keep up with the pack."

Human/Dog Translation: Now the way we're going to finish our five-step correction is this. After we have sharply tugged the leash, we're going to study the dog for five seconds. If he commits the same crime again, we're going to go right back to the beginning, to the first three steps: 1. *"NO!* 2. *Pause.* 3. *Snap and Release.* Then we're going to **(Step 4)** wait our five seconds, studying the dog intently. Assuming he's properly remorseful at the end of those five seconds, we go to on to the last step.

As we begin **(Step 5)**, we're going to feel the love and quietly say to the dog: "It's okay." We say this in a gentle, reassuring tone. Simply, "It's okay." We do NOT say something like "Oh, darling, I'm sorry I corrected you, can we be friends!" Just, "It's okay."

These five steps form the basis for solving any problem you encounter with your dog. They are steps that your dog will inherently understand at the basic, instinctual level, and you can use them successfully with only a little practice, patience, and persistence.

THE FIVE STEPS
TO SUCCESSFUL
TRAINING

1. NO!

2. PAUSE

3. SNAP—THEN RELEASE

4. WAIT FIVE SECONDS—OBSERVE
   RESPONSE

5. GENTLE REASSURANCE—
   "IT'S OKAY."

CHAPTER THREE

DO I WANT A DOG?

Of course you want a dog! You wouldn't be reading this book if you didn't want a dog or already have one. But stop a moment. You are going to have this dog for fifteen years! This is really a major commitment. I want you to go slow. Take your time. Do a little homework. It's a good idea, if you haven't thought about it before, to spend some time with dogs. Go to the park and watch people relating with dogs. Visit people who have dogs. Put yourself in their place. Visualize yourself doing what they do with their dogs. Walking. Grooming. Kenneling. Feeding. Cleaning up after the dog. These are things that you'll have to do and you might as well know about them before you start.

> Before you buy a dog, there are some practicalities you need to consider.

Owning a dog, sharing your life with a dog, is a wonderful thing. It adds years to your life. It keeps you more physically fit. Dogs are wonderful confidantes and counselors. They are a magical window to a wild and primitive past that we once shared—a time when the dog's life depended on us and our life depended on the dog. This is all beautiful. But if you don't have the temperament; if you don't have the patience; if you don't truly love dogs—then it might not be a wise choice for you.

Before you buy a dog, there are some practicalities you need to consider. Does your lifestyle allow you to properly care for a dog? Do you have the time for the dog? Will a dog "fit in" to your family?

If you have a family, invite friends who own a dog over for a visit. Ask them to bring the dog. Then you'll get to see your family relating  with the dog. You want every member of your family to pet the dog—to relate with the dog. You're trying to find out several things here. Is any member of my family afraid of the dog? Is any member of my family allergic to the dog? Is there anyone in the family who just "doesn't like" dogs?

Let me tell you a story about the heartbreaking experience an acquaintance of mine had. He had the home. He had the wife. He had a young son. In his mind the only thing missing was the dog. So, he got a beautiful mutt—a pit bull shepherd cross. And this was a marvelous animal. He brought it home. His son bonded with the dog instantly. Unfortunately, his son was also instantly allergic to the dog. My friend took his young son to the doctor. There he found out everything that it would take to have the boy and the dog co-exist without the boy being consumed by this rash that the dog gave him. My friend realized that he couldn't do it. And now he had to take the dog back. It was really tragic. It was a blow to his family.

So think about all these things. Do some homework. Relate with dogs, have them as part of your life. Visit people with dogs. Visualize yourself doing what they do with their dogs. And if all that makes sense to you and everything seems to indicate to you that there will be actually no problem in having a dog, then please go get one.

CHOOSING THE RIGHT
DOG FOR YOU

This is a very, very important part of your decision to have a dog. If you've followed my advice about deciding whether a dog will fit into your lifestyle, you've already spent a lot of time with dogs. And a picture of the animal that is perfect for you and your family is starting

> You need to spend time with the breed you think you'd like to own.

to form in your mind. Now what you can do at this point—let's say that you've decided that a yellow lab is perfect for you and your family—is contact the American Kennel Club to find out who breeds yellow labs in your area. Or, you can visit pet shops or even the local animal shelter. The point is this: you need to spend time with the breed of dog you think you'd like to own. You need to see how it matches with your family. You need to see how your family relates with the dog and see how the dog relates with your family.

Once you've narrowed your choice to a particular breed, do your research. Read up on the dog. Find ways to spend time with that particular breed. And, again, if you feel no mixed signals, if you discover nothing about this breed or about having this breed that would be detrimental to your lifestyle, and if you feel that you could offer this yellow lab an excellent life, then you've selected your dog.

I don't mean to rule out the mongrel as a candidate for your new puppy. Some of the best dogs that I've ever had in this long career of mine have been mongrels. Which brings us to the ways people come by dogs. There are several major ways. One of them, of course, is a private breeder. Now this individual may be representing a purebred line of dog—basset, beagle, golden retriever, whatever. It may be a particular breeding pair of mongrel dogs that creates these wonderful dogs that can't have any name other than mutt, but are still wonderful dogs and if you know about them and trust them then that's fine. There's also the pet shop, local animal shelter, and breed rescue organizations. So you have many choices to make when it comes to where you will find your new companion.

Let's talk about the pound first. It is a good thing to rescue a dog. The dogs that you find in the pound are on death row. And if you want to go over and try to save one, go right ahead. But I should caution you before you go to the pound that most of them have very strict rules for adoption. They're trying to do a good thing. The pound staff is trying to protect the dogs from being given to someone who will abuse them and trying to avoid releasing a dog to an abusive situation. (Sometimes pound dogs end up in research facilities or as "bait" for dog fights, so there is reason for caution.) Often, you have to jump through hoops to get a dog from the pound. If you have the patience to deal with them, then God bless you. Please go to the pound and save a dog.

When you go there, whether you're looking for a purebred dog or a mongrel, here's what you should do. Walk up and down the aisles, look at the dogs, try to feel what the dogs are about. Ask to spend some time with a particular dog or with one that's the type of dog you like. This is very important. Here we're getting into the electrical energy that I spoke about in Chapter 1. When you feel that energy coming to you from the dog, and the dog feels it coming from you, and each of you responds, then you probably have found the right dog for you.

It is possible to find the best friend you'll ever have in your whole life at the pound. But be careful! These dogs instinctively know that they'd better get out of there! So, walk up and down the cages. Leave yourself open. Feel the energy. Try to feel—granted, it is difficult in that environment—the energy of the individual dogs that you're passing by. Hunker down near an individual run and lean close and relate with the dogs you are attracted to. You will soon find the one that is meant to be "yours" if you trust your instincts and those of the dogs.

If you've already decided that you want a large dog, a small dog, or a scruffy little muttso, then walk around the pound until you find that dog. Walk up and down the aisles and leave yourself open. Try to find which dog really grabs you; which dog really appeals to you; which dog you really feel a camaraderie with. There is a tremendous communication going on between you and every dog that you pass.

If you find a dog that takes your fancy; if you see a dog and you say to yourself, "There it is—that's the scruffy little thing, or the large glossy thing, or the cute shaggy thing that I've been looking for!" Or if some dog just grabs your heart. If you look at this dog and say "I need to save this dog!" Then that's just a start. Don't fall for it—at least not yet!

Ask to spend time with the dog. Have them put a collar and leash on the dog and take it somewhere. Most pounds have an area where you can spend some time relating with the dog. Really get a feel for this dog. If you're bringing this dog home for your family, have your family with you. Be very calm. Be very quiet. Let the dog show himself to you. Be very loving, be very supportive. If you do find this dog—and it *can* happen—then go to them and say, "Yes, we want this dog."

Now this is just the beginning. They're going to put you through hoops. They're going to investigate your house, your yard; they're going to have you fill out questionnaires, sign guarantees of neutering. But if you have a chance, if you're willing to go through this, then what you're going to do is save this beautiful canine spirit from being killed. It's a good thing to do. Still, I feel compelled to say here that the standards by which dogs from the pound are released to adoptive homes need to be relaxed.

Thousands of wonderful animals get put down every year because potential owners are rejected. Shelter administrators decide they don't "have the right environment" for the dog. Most of these pounds will say that you have to have a fenced-in yard, you have to poison-proof your house, you have to prove a certain income level, you have to do all of these things before you can have a dog.

I've often thought that it would be interesting to go to the pound and pick one of the administrators and say: "You're going to be riffed—you are going to be unemployed as of the first of January. Now, because it's wintertime and you'll be unemployed, you might suffer discomfort, you might be homeless. So, to prevent you from experiencing those things, we're just going to kill you, okay?" Somehow, I don't think that particular administrator would agree with that—and yet that administrator would just as soon kill a dog as allow it to experience some regulator's idea of discomfort.

A friend of mine once was a barn carpenter. She had an early '50s panel truck, and what she did was travel the country and help people build barns (a very specialized form of carpentry). She had a beautiful old mongrel dog. In the truck, she had "her" place—the driver's seat—and the other bucket seat in the front was her dog's. In the back of the truck were tool cabinets, on the left, on top of which was her bed; on the right, more tool cabinets, with the dog's bed. The dog went everywhere with her. When she drove to work, she would park the truck, pop out the awning that was rolled up on the side, put the dog on a tie line with its food and water, and be working on the barn not 50 feet from the dog. On her lunch break she and the dog would play. In the evening she would either stay in the truck at the building site or go to a local park that allowed camping. The dog was never more than 50 feet from her, was catered to and pampered, and led the life of Riley. But the local humane society would not allow her to adopt a dog because she didn't meet the requirements. I think that's a crime.

Like my friend, there are lots of people living in apartments or living any one of a hundred thousand lifestyles who could offer a wonderful life to a dog, yet they are rejected as possible "adoptive parents" by the pound. A huge and terrible mistake. So, if you go to the pound and you make this magical connection with a dog and you pass their audition, then please do save a dog—from them!

So what's left? Private breeders and pet shops, which should both be held to the same high standards if you're getting a dog from them. What should you look for when you go to a pet shop? Let me give you an example based on an excellent shop that I know about, Potomac Kennels in Gaithersburg, Maryland. As you walk in the door you notice that the place is clean, well-organized, and pleasant. There is everything you could need for your dog or cat on display. There, on the far side of the room, behind a large plate-glass window are puppies on display. They are in well-ventilated kennels, each breed clearly identified.

If you are looking at puppies, it won't be long before a knowledgeable employee will help you. You can ask them any question about dogs and get an accurate answer. If a dog takes your fancy, they will bring him out, and you can go to a private room to play with the dog and get a first-hand feel for the animal's energy level and determine its temperament. Before they leave you alone with the puppy, they'll

counsel you on how handle him in a way that keeps the puppy safe.

If you decide to purchase the puppy, before you get out the door you will attend several classes on the best way to care for your new friend, and you will be supplied with anything you need to ensure your little friend's health, safety, and happiness. You will find out that each puppy is up to date on any vet needs, that you are given guarantees as to the puppy's future health. You will find out that they want to stay involved with you and your little chum for the rest of its life and help you in any way they can.

Sound good? It is. Unfortunately, there are many pet shops that do not maintain such high standards. These places usually sell "puppy mill" pets. Puppies that may not be healthy, properly socialized, or representative of their breed. So before you purchase a pet at your local pet shop, check carefully into where their puppies come from. And, if you have a sense that the object is to make as much money as possible off the pups, with the least amount of fuss, take your business elsewhere.

While the private breeder may not have a shop full of supplies, they should be offering you the same support, training in caring for your dog, and guarantees. Again, take your time and find a source of this quality. And, just because you are working with a "private breeder," don't make any assumptions. Check them out thoroughly to be sure they aren't running a puppy mill operation. Most quality breeders breed only one type of dog—Yorkies or Maltese or Cockers; German Shepherds, Retrievers, or whatever—and their goal is to improve the overall standard of the breed. If you get a puppy from one of these breeders you can be sure that they have provided your new pup with the best food and the best care and shelter. Some private breeders may have a very rustic barn-like facility—that's okay. Remember, these are the things you are looking for when you buy your puppy: dogs bred for health and temperament; their veterinary needs up to date; living in a clean, well-ventilated environment; and assurances of after-sale involvement.

Another place to look for a dog is a breed rescue group. These groups try to match up dogs with new owners when the "old" owner can no longer keep the dog. Sometimes it's because the owner has health problems or other personal problems that keep them from maintaining a home for their pet. And, sometimes, they have been unable to train this dog properly. It could be a housebreaking issue or the dog may be aggressive with children or other dogs. Or the dog may bark uncontrollably. In such cases, the rescue group will be sure you know about these problems before you adopt the dog, and often, they will give you hints on how to resolve them, as well. Sometimes, too, these groups are contacted by the local Humane Society when their particular breed is brought into the shelter or they may rescue dogs found at a puppy mill when authorities close it down.

Usually—but not always—the dogs you will find through rescue organizations are adult dogs of a particular breed, not puppies. Sometimes they have been abused or neglected, and it can take a while before they feel "safe" with you. But, if you have enough love and patience, and are willing to work on some behavior modification to eradicate bad habits they may have picked up in their old environment, this is an excellent place to find an AKC registered dog. Rescue organizations also have an application form that you must fill out and you must qualify in their eyes before they will let you adopt a dog. But usually a small donation and perhaps reimbursement for shots, spaying, or neutering is all they ask for by way of payment.

BEFORE YOU BRING YOUR DOG HOME

IMPORTANT NOTICE: BE SURE TO READ CHAPTERS 6 and 8
BEFORE YOU BRING YOUR NEW DOG HOME!

Are you ready? Well, probably not. But let's get things organized so our best friend comes home to an environment that he can settle into with a minimum of confusion, hair pulling, and hopping up and down. You are going to buy a lot

> Get things organized so our best friend comes home to an environment that he can settle into with a minimum of confusion.

of stuff for your puppy as time goes by, but make sure you have at least the following things when you bring your puppy home.

KENNEL CRATE

A plastic Vari-kennel is probably the best for your needs. A professional kennel operator might recommend a wire-constructed kennel.

But that has to do with a lot of issues related to quick clean-up and things of that nature that are more important to a professional with many dogs to handle and clean up after. As an owner of a single dog, you will find that the Vari-kennel offers several options that a wire kennel doesn't. First, the Vari-kennel is more den-like and your pup will feel safer and more comfortable in it. It's also airline approved so if you have to travel with the little guy you don't have to go through the added expense of buying one. It is also great to use when you want to take your dog with you in the car or when you need to transport him to your veterinarian. Before bringing your dog home, block off part of the crate with a cooler or milk crate so that puppy can stand up, turn around, lie down, and little else. This greatly helps in housebreaking.

FOOD AND WATER BOWLS

I think stainless steel bowls work best, but you can also use ceramic. Stay away from plastic bowls.

PUPPY FOOD

Iams, Eukanuba, and Nutro tend to offer the best quality nutrition, with high-quality ingredients. In my opinion, based on years of experience, Nutro is the best of these products.

But, be sure to find out what your puppy has been eating up to now, and at least initially continue using that food. When you begin to change over to the new food, mix a little of it with the old brand; each day increase the amount, until you have totally substituted the new food. This will keep your pup from experiencing any digestive problems, diarrhea, etc.

LEASH AND COLLAR

Buy a good-quality Nylon Adjustable Collar-no choke chains, please. You also will need a good-quality, 6-foot nylon leash. Make sure the leash is the appropriate weight for your dog.

ENZYMATIC CLEANSER

An enzymatic cleanser is used to clean up after "puppy accidents." It breaks down body wastes and eliminates odors. It also helps keep the pup from using the same spot to eliminate because it eliminates the scent that draws him there. Nature's Miracle works well, or you can use white vinegar.

OLD TOWELS

Set aside a few old towels to dry off the puppy's coat and feet when he comes in from the outside. Do NOT put towels in the crate— your puppy will use them for a bathroom.

Chew Toys

A few chew toys are a must, especially as puppies begin teething. Nylabones or gummabones are good, as are cow hooves. However, I must warn you about rawhide—it's possible for your puppy to chew and swallow a large enough chunk of rawhide to go through his stomach, lodge in his intestines and cause a blockage that can be fatal in just a few hours. It probably won't happen, but it can.

Brush

You can talk to the pet shop staff or the breeder about what type of brush to use on your dog. I have found that just a normal human hairbrush works really, really well on puppies.

You will probably discover you need or want some other items for your new dog as you go along, but these things will do for the first day. All right. Supplies are in the cabinet, food and water bowls are waiting! Let's take a quick look at the crate, then let's go get him.

Some schools of thought say that the crate should be placed away from everything and be kept in a secluded area so the puppy isn't bothered by noise and motion. Wrong! Dogs are pack animals. They do not need to be sent away from the pack to rest. They need to be part of the pack, at the very hub of activity.

Here they can see all that goes on and can be reassured that all is well. Also, you can correct them easily when there's any unnecessary vocalizing.

I think the kitchen is the best spot in the house for a crate. You can put it in a nook near the door and keep all the stuff that the puppy needs in a nearby cabinet. There's a handy sink and a tile floor for easy clean-up. A large crate can even give you some additional counter space. More importantly, all your puppy's needs are in one spot—food, water, the way outside, and his family.

Now one more reminder before you head out the door. As I said earlier, block off part of the crate so that there is just enough room for your new puppy to stand up, turn around, lie down, and little else. This strategy will be a great help when you start housebreaking the little guy. Okay. That's it. Now, let's head out.

BRINGING YOUR DOG HOME

Before you go to pick up your new dog, you should have taken care of all other business. You should have no other plans for the day but to pick your new dog up and bring him home. If you are single, have someone else drive you there if possible. (If not, be sure to take the new crate so you can transport him home safely.) If you are getting the dog for your family,

> Realize that it all starts now. As you begin this friendship you also are beginning to stablish yourself as Alpha.

take the whole family with you. Also, take a big towel, a leash, and a collar. Okay, now you're ready to pick up the dog and take him to his new home.

When you are ready to leave with the dog, follow these steps:

    1. Put on his collar, making sure it can't slip over his head. Remember to feel the love, the

joy, the anticipation of the adventure and remember to treat him with calm, loving hands.

2. As you reassure him with your voice, saying "it's okay," attach the leash and carry him outside.

3. Put him down and let him start exploring and going to the bathroom.

4. Start your new relationship off by immediately beginning to use the training procedures in this book.

Realize that it all starts right now. You and your best friend are together and you're sharing your first adventure. This is one of the most wonderful moments you will have in your long,

eventful friendship. As you begin this friendship you also are beginning to establish yourself as Alpha. Everything we talked about in Chapters 1 and 8 goes into use right away. So now, before you even leave the breeder, the pet shop, the pound, or the rescue group, this is how you begin to establish the right relationship with your new dog.

1. Let the puppy walk around outside for a few minutes, but if he pulls strongly, get a slack leash back with a tug. Pat your ankle eagerly and say "Right Here." When he gets there, pour on the love as you gently pull him against your leg, "Good Boy! Right Here! Good Boy!" You've begun!

2. So Let's Go. Patting your leg (say) "Let's Go puppy!" as you walk towards the car. "Good Boy! Let's Go!" Coax him and tug as you continue to say "Let's Go!" But, GO! Let him know right away that "Let's Go" means "we're going." Keep the leash slack except for tugs and snaps. When he comes along praise him—"Good Boy!" Be exuberant and proud of his progress.

3. When you get to the car, pat your ankle, saying, "Right Here!" It's a warm invitation to share bonding and love—not a command. Sit in the car with the big towel on your lap. Have the puppy handed to you and put him on your lap. Hold him close, be calm, and speak reassuringly. You're having fun! He'll feel that and have fun, too. His first car ride is a warm, loving, happy one. Oh, oh! He nips

you! "No!—Pause—Snap!" Wait 5 seconds, "it's okay!" Calm, quiet hand. Right back to the love.

Remember YOU are Alpha. His behavior modification is under way. It is a permanent part of your relationship. A continual flow—love, praise, encouragement; calm hands; and instant, remorseless correction—then right back to the love.

Now we're home. We'll wash the towel later. Put him down in the part of the yard that will be "his" or in the area where you intend to walk him. Let him sniff around. Explore. Give him time to "go potty." Take your time. Let him really check it out. Next, take him into the kitchen. Let him explore everything, saying often,"Good Boy! It's okay!" I would let him have access only to the kitchen and the family room area at first. You can allow him access to the rest of the house when you are confident of his housebreaking.

Let him inspect the crate that you used for transportation, which is now in his new home in the kitchen. Remember, your dog is by nature a pack animal. He needs to be at the very hub of activity in order to be reassured that all is well. Also, this is the easiest place to correct unnecessary vocalizing.

Now, sit on the floor. Call him over. Love, praise. Feel that at last you're home. He'll feel it too. Oops! He starts to pee! "NO! NO! NO!"—Snap!—Snap!—

Snap! Scoop him up, take him outside, calm him. If he pees outside offer him calm, loving praise (you know all this now). Puppy's home and you're on your way.

"IT'S OKAY"—A BASIC BUILDING BLOCK

The phrase, "It's Okay!" always means the same thing when you are working with your dog. It means it's all right, relax, it's over, take it easy. There's a group of canine behaviors that can be solved working with the phrase "It's Okay." That group includes noisy problems—barking, growling, whining, complaining, and guarding. You want your dog to do all of these things. You want him to tell you he wants to go to the bathroom. You want him to tell you someone's trying to pry the living room window open. You want him to vocalize and be part of your life. But you also want to be—and you really must be—in control.

> "It's Okay" always means the same thing when you are working with your dog. It means it's all right, relax, it's over, take it easy.

Particularly with the larger dogs, it's very important for you to be able to control their guarding tendencies. These dogs can get you in a lot of trouble and get themselves in trouble as well. Let's look at some specific times when "It's Okay!" can be used to put an end to a problem behavior.

IT'S OKAY/BARKING AND OTHER NOISY BEHAVIORS

Imagine you're in the kitchen making a pot of tea. From the living room you hear your dog going off. "Woof-woof-woof! Bark-bark-bark!" Now, you don't know what he's barking about, but your first response is to think: "Good Boy! You're watching! What is it?" You walk into the living room and you see that your dog is barking at a squirrel outside in a tree. Now to a dog, that squirrel is perhaps God's most perfect food. And he sees this unattainable thing, just out of reach, in the branches. At any rate, the squirrel is no threat to you, so there's no need for the barking to continue. And yet you do want the dog to bark when there is something he should bark at. Here's how we handle it.

RESPONSE 1

You say: "Good Boy, Spot!—But IT'S OKAY!" You say, "IT'S OKAY," in a forceful and commanding tone. (Notice that you praise him for the barking—"Good Boy!—but "IT'S OKAY!")

Now the first time you do this, that dog is going to look back at you as if to say "Yeah, right, Pops!" Then he'll get right back to the squirrel—"Woof-woof-woof."

RESPONSE 2

You now respond to his behavior like this:

❖ "NO!—Snap!—I said IT'S OKAY!"

If he barks again?

RESPONSE 3

Then, you respond again:

❖ NO!—Snap!—I said IT'S OKAY!"

What if your dog is guarding you or protecting you—he thinks this is a good and necessary thing he's doing for you. Well, if he's guarding you or protecting you and it's not necessary at that moment, you say to him:

❖ "GOOD BOY, Fang!—But IT'S OKAY!"

If he continues, at the next menacing step, growl, or threat, repeat the command, then act on it:

❖ "NO!—Snap!—I said IT'S OKAY!

In a very short time your dog will realize that when you say to him in a commanding tone "IT'S OKAY!" it's time for that vocalizing to stop. You now have control barking, growling, whining, complaining, guarding. Easy, isn't it?

IT'S OKAY/CRATE TRAINING ISSUES

All right now we have control of barking, growling, whining, complaining and guarding. One of the

first opportunities to address these issues will probably come up when you introduce your dog to his
crate/kennel. The first thing you need to realize as far
as kenneling (crating) your dog goes, is that YOU
have to feel good about it. Remember the electrical
energy you're radiating? If you feel good about that
kennel, so will the dog. And if you've made sure that
all of his needs are met and that there's no reason for
him to be uncomfortable in the kennel, then when
you put him in the kennel and he starts to bark, you
can say to him "Fi-DO, IT'S OKAY!" Next peep,
"NO!" and then thump the top of the crate (kennel)
twice (BUMP!BUMP!), "I said, IT'S OKAY!" He com-
plains some more. You say NO!—BUMP!BUMP!—I
said, IT'S OKAY!" Very quickly he will realize that
you feel good about the crate and when he's in the
crate you want him to be quiet.

IT'S OKAY/BOUNDARY ISSUES

Now there's a final category of immediate issues
that we need to cover in establishing our right relationship and that's boundaries. What are the boundaries? Front door, back door, car doors, the windows
of your house, car windows, and the line around
your property. These are all lines that your dog
should never ever cross without permission. Most
dogs that die of something besides old age die of
crossing one of those lines. So we're serious about
this.

Let's take the front door, for example. Because, you see, the metal strip across the bottom of your front door is a line, or a boundary, if you will, that your dog should never cross without permission. Most schools on dog training are going to tell you that as you're opening your dog you should say: "Wait. Stay back! Stay in!" (or something like that). That's good, except for that day when you're busy and you're not thinking about the dog. So you open the door. You're late to work and you've got to get out the door. But the dog isn't busy, he's watching. And he records the fact that you didn't say those "Stay in!" words. "Zoom!" out the door he goes, into the street. God knows what could happen to him there.

There's a better way. You teach your dog to respect the boundaries by training him not to cross them EVER until you have given him permis-sion. Here's how it works. Put your dog on leash. Walk him down the hallway. The front door and the storm door are wide open. Okay. You just stand there. Don't say a word. If he tries to cross that metal strip to

go outside, you respond with "NO!—SNAP!" and, Boom!, you snap him back in. If he tries again, "NO! SNAP!" and you snap him back in. Now you'll see you have a dog, sitting in your hallway, looking at the metal strip, looking at you as if to say "Okay, I've got it. I don't cross the metal strip."

The next step in this little drill is that you now, being very careful not to put any pressure whatsoever on that collar, slowly back through the door. You're holding the leash in your left hand. If he tries to follow you through the door, you say "NO!" and you snap him back in. He tries to follow you out again "NO!" and you snap him back in. You see, now you have a dog who's trying desperately to get away from that door.

Now that you are standing outside and he is standing, or sitting, inside and very clearly not attempting to cross that door, you can let him start for the door, saying "Let's Go!" and patting your thigh twice, nice firm pats, again you say, "Let's Go!" But the only way he gets out of any door is this. You open the door, step through first, and he doesn't cross that threshold or come out through that car door, until you say: "Let's Go!"

Now I don't mean to suggest that you spend the rest of your life opening the door, standing there, stepping through it, standing there some more, and then saying "Let's Go!" That just won't be the case. You see your dog will learn this very, very quickly. So after a little training, the way it really works is this: you go down the hallway, you open the door, you see that the dog has very clearly stopped right there— you're still moving, he's stopped—and you say "Let's Go!" In other words, someone watching from ten feet away would see you moving smoothly through the door and him following right with you. But you would have seen him stop; and you would know he would have waited, until you said "Let's Go!"

To make this behavior completely sharp, what you do is, this. Periodically you walk through that door without saying "Let's Go!" If he attempts to fol- low you "NO! (Boom) SNAP!" and you snap him back in. In this way we are going to save our dog from the most common death besides old age and that is bolting out of a door, bolting out of the yard, and bolt- ing into the street filled with traffic and death. Leave your dog in the car for a few minutes, then open the car door. If he tries to jump out without permission, "bark and snap" him back in until he waits for the words "Let's Go." Walk him around your property line. Every time he crosses the line, you say NO! And snap him back. Teach him he can **NEVER** step out of your yard until you've said "Let's Go."

So, to summarize, we use the five-step correction, that, believe me (and we will discuss this further in behavior modification) will cure 99 percent of what your dog does wrong. Remember, that (five-step) cor- rection is quite simply the following:

1. No!
2. Pause
3. Snap—then release
4. Wait five seconds (observe response)
5. Gentle reassurance, in the form of "It's Okay" in a gentle, reassuring tone.

Remember, when it's time for barking, growling, whining, complaining, or guarding to stop, we indicate this to the dog by saying "Good Boy (or Girl), It's Okay! With the next bark, growl, or menacing step, its NO! SNAP. I said It's Okay!

And, finally, remember that your dog must never cross any boundary (and those are front door, back door, car doors, house windows, car windows, and the line around your property.) Your dog must never cross any one of those lines unless you have first stepped across the line and then said "Let's Go!" If he crosses any one of those boundaries without permission it's "NO! SNAP!" and he's back in.

USING ‛THE WARNING TONE‛

Now coupled with this praising and correcting is the "warning tone." The warning tone is the elevation of the end of the dog's name or the second syllable of the dog's name. (Please do not name your dog "Mesopotamia" or "Myocardial Infarction"!) A simple two-syllable or one-syllable name really works. When we elevate the end of the dog's name as in

"Fi-DO! or "Bow-ZER!" or "Plu-TO," we are warning him. That warning means three things:

❖ Number 1: "You are about to do the wrong thing, in which case I'm going to nail you" (with one of the corrections).

❖ Number 2: "Bow-ZER, you've gone too far. (Twenty, thirty, forty feet; it's far enough. Stop there.")

and finally,

❖ Number 3: "Bow-ZER, I'm about to give you a command."

You'll find yourself saying this warning tone in different ways. More threatening for a warning; more crisp and inviting at the beginning of an obedience command. But at any rate, in all three cases it means "Stop and look!"

You see Bowser trotting towards you with "I'm going to jump on you" written all over him; you say "Bow-ZER!" At first he'll ignore you and it won't mean anything. But when he ignores "Bow-ZER!" and he jumps and gets corrected, very quickly he'll realize "when I hear that warning tone I better think—oh, right, I don't jump" and he will turn away.

Your dog will stop and turn and look at you when you say his name like that. And of course when we say "Bow-ZER!" at the beginning of a command it means "we're not negotiating now, you're working." In all cases it means "Stop and look!" To ignore the warning tone is to surely lead to correction. And let me tell you something, within one year of the time you've read the sentence that you're reading right now, your dog will be running towards certain death and you'll have no time to say anything else but "Bow-ZER!" He will stop and turn, and the trash truck that was just about to run over him will pass him by, and he'll be alive and unharmed. So this warning tone is very, very important. As he approaches a boundary that he's not supposed to cross, "Bow-ZER!" He should stop and turn, rather than cross the boundary. And when he DOES stop and turn; when he DOES look at you when you say "Bow-ZER!" your job, as Alpha, is to praise him.

So now we have learned how to give our warning, we've learned how to give the five-step correction, worked on our correction for vocalizing or guarding and on our boundary training. Believe me. It's as easy as this. We are well on our way to establishing a beautiful relationship with this dog. Next we will talk about how to use these techniques for behavior modification.

BEHAVIOR MODIFICATION/ HOUSEBREAKING

Let me begin by saying that it's very important to remember everything we read in Chapter 1 about how wolves keep order in the pack as we proceed with behavior modification. Using a leash, the simple "Let's Go, Right Here" commands and your dog's instinctual need to obey the Alpha, I am going to show you how to teach your puppy to "do the right thing" at all times. And I'm going to give you two nearly fool-proof methods for housebreaking your dog. One involves the leash; the other his crate.

> The young puppy would begin his life with me living in one of two conditions: (1) in his crate or (2) on the leash.

I'll tell you what I would do if I had just brought a young puppy home and I was going to raise him and he was going to be one of my dogs. That young puppy would begin his life with me living in one of two conditions. He would either be (1) in his crate or (2) on the leash. And that leash would be either on my wrist or I would be holding it.

Everywhere I went I would say to him "Plu-TO, Let's Go!" patting my hip twice firmly, and off I'd go! Now, he may think "but I'm watching Lassie." SNAP! "Ooh, jeez! I guess we're going!" When you say "Let's Go!" he goes. Now, if he's hesitating or lagging behind, remember, he's putting stress on that leash. Your response is to tug him up, get him going: "Let's Go!" And, when he starts moving with you, your response is "That's it! Good Boy! Now you're work-ing. Let's Go! Good Boy!" Every time you change directions, "Let's Go!" Every time you move from one room to the next, "Let's Go!"

The puppy quickly learns that you insist on a slack leash. And that means that he has to focus on you. In order to keep that leash slack, he has to watch you, watch what you're doing and stay with you—and

that's a good thing. Now while we're "Let's Go-ing!" about the place, what we're going to do periodically is stop. We're not patting our thigh firmly now and saying "Let's Go!" in this sort of commanding voice—what we're actually doing now is leaning down and patting our calf and saying "Good Boy! Right Here, Right Here!" What that means is he is to come over, and he will, by the way, because what we are doing is very inviting. We gently pat our leg (pat-pat-pat) "Right Here. Good Boy!"

What is it that we want this puppy to do? He is to come and lean against us, while we gently pull him against our leg in a gentle caress. We don't pull him over with the leash—we invite him over by patting our calf, saying in a gentle voice "Right Here!" When he gets close we kind of scoop him against us. That's the nicest thing that's ever happened to him. "Right Here!" is his reward for obeying a "Let's Go!" And this is a curious thing. The thing we actually want most from a dog is for him to come and be with us when we call him. Think about it. Well, that's his reward for obeying a "Let's Go!" Insidious, isn't it. At any rate, so we're moving around, going through our life "Let's Go! Right Here! Good Boy!" and he's learning to be with us and out of our way.

All this time he is on his leash, attached to your wrist. And, believe me, you can reach the tallest cabinet in the kitchen, you can operate the computer, you can go out and change the oil in the tractor, the dog is learning to be with you and out of your way at the same time you're engaging in every household activity. Meanwhile, he can't do one single thing wrong without your being aware of it! You're walking along and he nips your ankle. You don't have to look for a leash—it's right there! "NO!" Snap! Wait five seconds. Gentle reassurance, "It's Okay." And, on we go.

HOUSEBREAKING USING THE LEASH

Now here's how the leash works when it comes to housebreaking. If you have your puppy on a leash and he decides to use your house for a bathroom—well, he can't zip around the corner of the sofa, go to the bathroom, and come back looking at you like "what, I didn't do nuttin'!" Because he's on the leash, he'll have to try to go to the bathroom right in front of you. And, of course, as soon as you see his body starting to form into the posture of a dog that's going to the bathroom, your response: "NO! NO! NO! NO!" Then, Snap-Snap-Snap, and hustle him outside real quick.

You new little puppy will quickly realize a very important fact of life: "My God, I can't go to the bathroom in here—every time I even start to try they bark 'NO' and bite me (Snap!) in the neck! I can't get away with that. I've got to hold myself forever!" Now, eventually the day will come that no matter how hard he's trying to hold himself, he will realize "I'm going to go to the bathroom and they're going to beat me up." Of course, you're not beating him up—it's ritualistic—yet he'll regard it as being firmly corrected. What he'll do is look at you and complain about his upcoming punishment. He'll look at you and whine as if to say "you're going to beat me up!" You'll say, "Good Boy. Let's Go!" And you take him right outside, and he goes to the bathroom and believe me, they do pick this up! "My gosh, I complained about my upcoming beating (punishment) and I don't get it, but they take me outside and I get to go potty outside!"

I want you to stop for a moment and think about this. We've got a dog that's learning to go with us—now there are six feet of leash, three feet of arm—basically, about nine feet—where he can be around us while he's in "Let's Go" mode, as long as there's no pressure on the leash. So, he's learning to move smartly with us and to focus on us when we say "Let's Go!" He's learning to trot over and enjoy this beautiful bonding love when we say "Right Here!" He's learning he can't get away with anything because he's instantly corrected for it. And, he's learning that he has to hold his bowels and bladder (he has to build up that bowel and bladder strength) and learning to tell us he has to go to the bathroom. Now that's a heck of a lot of advantage for the inconvenience of having this dog on the leash. And believe me, you CAN engage in almost any activity while having that leash either in your hand or around your wrist.

BACK TO BASICS

Now here's how this formula works. When it's been a few days—and I don't know, it might take ten days, it might take a little bit longer. But when it's been a few days since there's been any pressure on that leash—because he hasn't tried to go to the bathroom in the house, he hasn't tried to bite anything or get in the trash, he's responded smartly to "Let's Go!" and "Right Here!"—in other words, when he's been a perfect little puppy, or as perfect as puppies get. What we do is DROP the leash.

That's the next step in training your puppy: you drop the leash. Now what happens here is that he's still expected to do everything the same, it's just that we're not going to hold the leash. So, quick scenario here.

You're in the living room and you decide to go to the kitchen to make a pot of tea, and you say, "Plu-TO! Let's Go!" And he looks at you as if to say "Huh! Well, I can tell you're not holding the leash! So, why should I listen to you!" Your response: Walk back, pick up the leash, give it a sharp tug, get him motivated. Say, "Let's Go!" and as you start to move along together smartly, you drop the leash, and as he's moving along beside you, you say: "Good Boy, Pluto!"

You get to the kitchen, "Right Here!" He leans against you, you start making the pot of tea. He starts to wander off, remember the warning tone "Plu-TO!" He should stop—if he doesn't, step on the leash. Now he's stopped and you say, "Right Here! Good Boy!" Again, he's learning to stop and look when he hears the warning tone and he's learning that it doesn't make any difference that you're not holding the leash. You actually still have one.

After a few more days—and, again, I don't know how long; I've had it take as little as a week—but, when it's been a few days since you've had to pick the leash up, you take the leash off! What I do in this situation, is wear the leash on my neck so that I don't have to go looking for it and he can see it. Now the same scenario. I'm in the living room and I'm going to the kitchen to make a cup of tea. I say to him "Pluto, Let's Go!" and he looks at me as if to say "Well, there's no leash on me. Why should I listen to you!" And now he discovers the ultimate horrible truth— you're going to walk back and attach the leash! Snap him up! "Let's Go Boy!" And off you go towards the kitchen.

You drop the leash, but you keep the leash on him for just a short time. Then, watch him, take the leash off, and pick up where you left off—with him responding to "Let's Go!" and responding to "Right Here!" and being right with you and listening to his warning tone—all with no leash on him. And see, what you have here is a "Let's Go!" "Right Here" puppy that understands he's not going to get away with anything, that's holding himself like mad and telling you he's got to go to the bathroom, and *he's not on a leash!*

Now you can use this same technique outside as well. Every time you take him for a walk, as you're moving along, you say "Let's Go!" Periodically, during every walk, stop and say "Right Here! Good Boy!" If there's a distraction across the street and he starts to look at it—say, in the warning tone, "Plu-TO!" "Right Here!" "Good Boy!" If he doesn't respond, give him a little tug—"Pluto! Right Here!" and then he comes over and he gets this wonderful reward "Good Boy!" You'll see that very, very quickly while you may be holding that leash while he's outside, you're not actually using it.

There is another method that is useful here, especially for outdoor work. It requires about 50 feet of clothesline. You can buy lunge line at about a dollar a foot, but 50 feet of clothesline at $2.50 works just as well and is a lot cheaper.

By now your pup understands that when you're on a walk it's "Let's Go!" and "Right Here!" on a regular basis. Now, you stretch the 50 feet of clothesline out, someplace—in your yard, at the park, in a field, or whatever. Take him to the 50 feet of clothesline and tie the line to his leash (which is attached to his collar) and drop the line. You are now out in the middle of nowhere and you're not holding anything, but you ARE standing on the clothesline.

Now begin doing exactly the same thing you have been doing when you worked on leash in the house and on walks. Say: "Plu-TO, Let's Go!" Then, you start walking down the clothesline—walking on the clothesline. Pluto might look at you as if to say, "Oh, wait a minute, we're out in the middle of nowhere and you're not holding anything! Why would I listen!" That's when you say, "Plu-TO!" If he ignores you, reach down, keeping your hand close to the ground, give that clothesline a sharp tug—Snap!— and say: "I said, Let's Go!"

What a surprise! You've just "bitten him on the neck" from 30 feet! He's impressed. So he understands "Let's Go!" He understands "Right Here!" And now you're out in the middle of a park someplace, and you still have positive control of him.

I've used this method a thousand, thousand times. You can take him for walks like this. Once he understands the basics of "Let's Go" and "Right Here" you can actually stretch out that 50 feet of line and take him for a walk around the neighborhood, take him for a walk in the park. You're not touching anything. He starts to get a little bit ahead: "Plu-TO!" He stops—"Good Boy! Plu-TO! Right Here!" And he trots right back to you. If he doesn't, you give him a "Snap!" You'll see in a very short time that you haven't been using that line at all.

There's another variation here. You take your pooper scooper or your plastic bag and you go to a double tennis court somewhere. (The reason for the pooper scooper or the plastic bag is you want to be polite to the tennis players and make sure you don't leave any mess.) Now, step into that tennis court and work him on that 50-foot line for a while, then take it off. You'll see that you have this dog in this wide open space doing exactly what you ask him to do. Now you have a dog that you can predictably count on. Now isn't this obedience? Well, while this isn't a formal obedience command, it is the way to a very, very good relationship with your dog. With only a "Let's Go!" and "Right Here!" the two of you are moving freely through life.

Let me describe a scenario for you. Let's say, your dog learns nothing more than this. Now, you've decided that you want to go for a walk, you want to walk around the park for a while, then go to your favorite sidewalk café. So here you go. (Of course, you've got your leash in your back pocket.) You say to him, "Plu-TO! Let's Go!" And off the two of you go. And you're walking around, you're having a ball, you're playing fetch—but, oh-oh!, here comes a guy on a bicycle! "Plu-TO! RIGHT HERE!" He immediately trots over and leans against you. You share this beautiful, bonding affection. When the biker's gone by, it's "Good Boy, Pluto! Now Let's Go!"

You walk to your favorite sidewalk café, sit down at the table, "Plu-TO, Right Here!" he leans against you, sees the chair, the table, and thinks "Whoa! This action's going to take about 45 minutes!" So he plops down for a nap. Anybody watching you that didn't know any better would swear that your dog is immaculately trained. But you would know that he's just had the most basic training. A little aside here: I find that I do use the formal obedience commands with all of my dogs, but it really gets down to more use of "Let's Go!" and "Right Here!" than anything else.

HOUSEBREAKING USING A CRATE

In the beginning of this chapter, I promised to give you two foolproof methods for housebreaking your dog. (And, by the way, these methods work just as well for adult dogs as they do for puppies.) We talked about a formula for when he's out of the crate. Next, I'm going to give you a very specific and predictable procedure and schedule for housebreaking your dog using a crate.

Let me begin by saying this—It's not cruel to confine your dog in a crate. Little puppies need 16 hours a day of sleeping anyway, and you don't want them to be active all the time because their little bones are growing and knitting and all these puppy-growing things, and they actually need a lot of rest. Don't feel bad about having your dog in the crate. What I'm going to describe to you is what I've found to be the best way to housebreak a dog. Before we get started though, I want to dispel a couple of myths.

The first one is that a dog doesn't have a memory past 35 seconds. This myth implies that if you don't catch the dog in the act, or within 35 seconds of the time it committed some sort of a crime, you can't correct him because he has no idea of what he's done. That is a huge and terrible misconception. Dogs have excellent memories. They can remember a single incident from early puppyhood until tottering old age. In fact, if you've owned a dog before you probably know this.

Let's say, for example, that you are away from home for eight or ten hours. If he's done nothing wrong while you've been gone, he's right there at the door wagging his tail "Hi! Glad to see you!" when you get home, right? But let's say you come home and he's not right there to greet you. You see him and think: "Why, for heaven's sake, is he sitting in the corner of the living room, with his head down, casting sheepish, sidelong glances at me?" I'll tell you why. He's done something wrong! And not only that, he remembers what he did; he remembers that you don't like it; and he remembers that you're going to be mad. Sorry, experts from Harvard or wherever, but the fact is that anyone who's owned a dog knows they have excellent memories—well past 35 seconds!

If you want to test this "theory" sometime when you come home and see your dog behaving like he did something wrong, try doing what I always do. I look at the dog and say "All right, you, where is it?" The poor dog can't help himself! He'll look at that third bedroom on the left and back at you like "What!" Now I don't know what "it" is—it might be a torn up pillow or a pile of poop—but I do know that in that third bedroom on the left a crime has been committed. If you need more proof, make the test even more accurate. Put the leash on the dog walk him away from that "third bedroom on the left." Watch him. He's wagging his tail and looks really happy. Now, turn toward that room and move closer and closer to the scene of the crime. As you reach the door, he'll be backing up—"Don't go in there! Don't do it!"—proving very clearly that he remembers what he did. Think about it. If he soils the carpet or his crate, if he's in there with a pile of poop—come on—do you really believe that he thinks the poop fairy brought it? Of course not! He knows that he did it. He's acutely aware of it. So you CAN correct him for it. So much for the 35-second theory!

Next, a word about water. The vet will tell you that your dog has to have access to water 24 hours a day. I think that is a great cruelty. If your puppy is continually loading his bladder with water, he's going to continually have to pee. If he gets water only with his meals, he'll be just fine. I've been doing this for many years, and I can assure you that I've never had a dog die of thirst between breakfast and dinner or between dinner and breakfast.

Here's a quick "experiment" that might help you understand why they shouldn't have water 24 hours a day. Drink a six pack of cheap beer, then go stand in a phone booth. See how long you can last in the phone booth before you are in agony. Well, if you give your dog free access to water you're doing exactly the same thing to him. So food and water with meals only. If you take him for a walk somewhere and he appears to be thirsty, give him a couple of ice cubes. Ice cubes are a good treat and they satisfy the cooling of his throat and his need to feel a sensation of liquid. You won't be harming the dog if he has food and water at his mealtimes only. There are all kinds of parallels in nature that will bear me out on this. I've never seen attendants with bowls of water following wolf packs around in the "North Woods." And, African hunting dogs often drink twice a day and that's it. So, your dog is made of the same stuff. He will be fine, and he will adjust.

There's one more thing I need to point out before moving on to the housebreaking process. Certain puppies, especially the smaller ones, like Silkies and Yorkies, Maltese, and other small breeds, may have special dietary needs. In other words, you're going to have to monitor their electrolyte levels a lot more closely. Those specific dogs shouldn't be on a two-meal-a-day schedule. These dogs are few and far between and you will be cautioned about this by the breeder, pet store, or rescue operation before you ever take the dog home. Ninety-nine out of a hundred dogs can be on the housebreaking schedule I'm going to describe. For dogs that do need this constant monitoring of electrolyte levels and other eating-related issues, just incorporate those needs into developing a workable schedule.

Now, back to crate training. The first thing you need to do is set up a schedule. I'm going to pick an arbitrary time. Let's say, you get up at 7:00 a.m. You want some time to interact with the dog, maybe play with it. Then you plan to take care of his needs and go to work. Here's a very good housebreaking schedule. You get up at 7:00 and slip into your dog walking clothes. Go to the crate. If you come to a clean, dry crate, don't make a big deal out of this now, but as you're opening the crate's door, and smoothly clipping on the leash, and moving toward the door, you say to him softly "What a Good Boy! Let's Go!" and out the door you go.

Now, theoretically, he's held himself all night. So he's going to go right away. He's going to have to go and he will. You bring him back in. Next you give him one-third of his daily food (let's say he's supposed to get a cup and a half a day—well he gets a half a cup of dog food) and an equal amount of water in a separate bowl. You give him ten minutes and ten minutes only to eat that food and drink that water. You can sit there and have a cup of coffee while he eats his food. After ten minutes you pick the food and water up whether he's finished or not. This is important, because you want to create a dog that realizes he only has so much time to eat.

After you take up the food, you put him in the crate for half an hour. Now during this half hour, you're running around and getting your stuff done, your morning stuff, whatever you have to do to get yourself ready for work. At the end of that half hour you take him out for a second chance to go to the bathroom. Don't make a big deal out of this now. He's got to realize "this is what I'm out here for." You bring him back in and put him in the crate "Pluto! Kennel! What a Good Boy!" followed by "It's Okay!" And now you're off to work. Because he's only had one-third of his food and the same amount of water, he doesn't have that big a load to hold as he goes through his day.

When you return from work, the process is very similar. Theoretically, he's been able to hold himself. So, you come to the crate—and again, don't make a big fuss or a big deal about it, like saying, "Boy! I've missed you!" Just walk up to the crate and say, "Hello Pluto! What a Good Boy!" While you're saying this, you smoothly clip on the leash. The you pick him up get him outside. As you go through the door, you should be saying, "Let's Go!" No hesitation here. If he's held himself all day, he's got to go, and he's going to go right away. Bring him back in, give him the other two-thirds of his food and all the water he wants. But leave them down for <u>ten minutes only.</u> And now, again, you wait for half an hour

During the half-hour wait, your dog can either be in the crate or—because you're home, awake, and watching—he can be out of the crate. If he's out of the crate, keep his leash on your wrist or hold it. As we said before, this keeps your puppy out of trouble and provides you with an early warning system if he starts to "have an accident." After half an hour you take him out again and give him another chance to go to the bathroom.

I recommend keeping him out of the crate at this point. But remember that at least initially during this process you have him on the leash. This way he can't run off and have a little accident and come back—he's either going to have to tell you that he's got to go to the bathroom or he's going to go in front of you and get corrected for it. This is how we help him build his bowel and bladder control.

Give him his final walk for the day just before he goes to bed. He's had his "play time" from let's say 4:30, 5:00 o'clock when you come home. He's been walked and fed. He's had from 5:00 o'clock 'til 10:30 or 11:00 or so to process all that food and water. And now he's going to bed with mercifully empty bowels and bladder.

What this schedule does is help adjust your dog's metabolism to the intake of food and water at specific times and the processing of this food and water at certain times. This very predictable schedule "sets" the pup's body clock and greatly enhances and eases the housebreaking process. When he's really got it down, of course, you can be a little bit more relaxed. But it's such a handy thing for your dog to realize he's got three cardinal walking times. Walk/food/walk in the morning, walk/food/walk at the earliest possible time in the afternoon, and a final walk just before bed. Once he's on that schedule you can live your life and share quality time with your dog, and he will be much happier as a result of it.

In the middle of all this control and training and processing of the dog, there's something else we must realize. He does need his time to be Pluto the carefree, chaotic puppy. He just doesn't need all that much of that. A few little breaks, ten minutes or so at a time, in which he's absolutely free to tear up and down and have a ball, that's all he really needs, say two or three times a day. And he can drag the leash with him while he's doing that. So, you're throwing him a ball, playing with him and his pull toy, and he's hopping around and scampering and being a nut. But while he's doing this, watch him very carefully, and be ready to step in at a moment's notice. Now, when I say step in, I mean step on that leash to immobilize him, then pick it up and take control. If he's having a housebreaking accident or if he's decided to chew up on the sofa, whatever, it's up to you to stop him. So let him have those crazy times a few times a day. But watch him like a hawk during those times and be ready to resume control at a moment's notice.

CHAPTER NINE

OBEDIENCE

Before I start this chapter, there's something I must share with you. Imagine this scene. It's mid-September, about 11:30 at night, and almost a full moon. The dogs and I are out for a run. Seven dogs and myself, by the river, through the woods, a pack on the prowl. We run in perfect, joyful harmony. "Let's Go! Right Here!" A joyful celebration of our unity and our shared love of life. Now we're all back at the kennel. Not one obedience command was given.

> Obedience is the best way to lead your pack.

You, too, can have this. But dogs do need obedience. If you've done everything in Chapters 1 through 8, you now have a happy, healthy, much-loved puppy who views you as his leader, fun-provider, counselor, confidant, hero, and all-around swell person. In short, you're Alpha! And, what do Alphas do? They lead the pack. Obedience is the best way to lead your pack. It adds years to your dog's life by satisfying his need to work. It also adds years to his life because with obedience you can call him back from something that would surely kill him. Or in the case of some dogs, call him back from something they would surely kill.

Working with your dog on obedience is different from "Let's Go" and "Right Here." "Let's Go" and "Right Here" are free and spontaneous, even though the dog still must do that. Obedience is different in that now there is no negotiation. This is your dog's work. Here are the basics.

We use our warning tone "Plu-TO!" When you elevate the second syllable, you are warning your dog; telling him, "You are now working." You do not repeat commands. The dog has one chance and one chance only to obey an obedience command. Now, we don't do this to be stern or to show off. We do this because in the time it takes to repeat an obedience command the dog could die. So we are doing this because we love and respect the dog and we desire his success. And because we're doing this out of love, there's no anger, there's no fear, there's no frustration. Because we are doing this out of love we are tireless.

The dog will feel that you are doing this out of love. The dog will feel that, "well, my Alpha clearly wants me to do this and he wants me to do it right now. I can feel the love, I can feel the encouragement, but I can also feel that he is *ab-so-lutely* serious about this and there will never be negotiation." Keep this attitude firmly in mind when you work with your dogs in obedience. As you practice working with your dog, you will get better at giving commands, and he will get better at obeying them.

As with all training, start on leash, work toward a dropped leash, and finally you will use no leash at all. As you and your dog master each command, you will add the next one to your workout, steadily increasing the number of commands until all five—Sit-Stay, Come-Stay, Down-Stay, Heel, and Place-Stay—are included in the workout.

You should have one formal, structured workout for 10 minutes every day. The most valuable workout, however, is the quick, blitz workout. This comes to the dog at any hour of the day or night, inside, outside, at the park, weddings, bar mitzvahs, anywhere! This teaches your young puppy that obedience can be needed at a moment's notice, out of the blue, with no warning at all. And, if you think about it for a moment, that's when you're really going to need obedience.

We must feel good about what we're doing. This good feeling is reflected in our body language and our vocal tone. If we have the slightest doubt, the dog will know it and our ability to train him will be diminished. We create interest, excitement, and authority with clear, concise, energetic delivery of commands, mixed with loving encouragement, oceans of praise, backed with instant, stern correction. Now, let's start learning how to give your dog the proper commands and what to do to make sure he obeys them.

SIT-STAY

Everything we've done so far has been designed to welcome our special friend into a warm, loving, well-structured environment that meets all of his physical and psychological needs. It is my hope that at this time the spiritual aspect of the man-dog relationship is there also. There is an ancient, wild magic here that cannot be explained in physical terms alone. As we go through this obedience program, please be aware that using these commands can be likened to using the controls to an airplane. On the

> There is an ancient, wild magic here that cannot be explained in physical terms alone.

one level we're just pushing buttons and pedals, on the other hand we're flying. Enough of that. Let's roll up our sleeves and get to work!

Let's feel good, let's get excited! We click on the leash (or pick it up) and say, "Bowser, are you ready?" We've just turned on the motor. "Let's Go! Good

Boy!" Change direction, "Let's Go!" Good Boy!" and "Right Here!" "Oh, Good Boy!" Now that he's leaning against us and we're close, we're going to slide the clasp of the leash where it attaches to the collar so that it's under his neck. We're going to hold the leash in our left hand, about three feet from his neck. Keeping the clasp under his chin, we're going to back up very slowly, and say softly, gently "Let's Go!"

Now, we straighten our left arm to keep some distance from him, then we stop and say "Bow-SER!" and pointing the index finger of the right hand like a toy gun, right between his eyes, we step towards him saying "Sit!"

Use a sharp, sharp, clipped stage whisper. As you step forward, thrust your hand signal forward to about three feet from his face. This warning tone, step forward, hand thrust, "Sit!" combination should sit him.

If after this, he DOES-N'T sit, tug the leash sharply up until it's at a forty-five degree angle. His instinct will be to resist this pressure. In order to do this he will have to align his spine at a forty-five degree angle to the ground. When a dog's spine is at that angle, he is sitting. His resistance has served us. Insidious, aren't we.

Now, just like a cop stopping traffic, we thrust that flat palm at him and say "Stay!" Short, clipped, stage whisper. Then "Good Boy!" Next, a gentle caress, and you say, "Stay!" "Good Boy!" And, another gentle

STAY

caress. We praise him softly so he doesn't feel like he's being punished, but finish our praise with "Stay!" If he moves, it's "No!" And we use an upward snap, and "Stay!" "That's it! Good Boy! Stay!" He may try to move several times. Each time, you use: "No!"— Snap!—"Stay!"

When he is stable, stalk around him slowly, saying "Stay!" Make sure that the leash stays still as you walk back and forth. When he is still and stable, stand straight and tall, hand thrust out in "Stay!" This posture does not invite him over. Then bend forward at the waist and turn your hand palm up as you say "Take a break!" Pat your calf! Say "Right Here! Good Boy! Right Here!" and praise him like mad.

Then, "Are you ready? Let's Go! Good Boy! Right Here!" Position leash, step back, "Let's Go!" Step

TAKE A
BREAK

forward, "Bow-SER! Sit! Stay!" "Good Boy!" Have him hold the stay for a while, correct him as needed, then "Take a break!"

If you say "SIT," and he drops into a lie-down position, pull him up into a sit and say "Stay!" If he drops again put your fingertips under his collar, under his chin, pull him into a sit, hold him there and say "Stay!" "Good Boy!" "Stay!" Slowly relax pressure as you say "Stay!" in a stage whisper. Then proceed as we did initially. *Don't push his rump down with your hand!*

All this is done with pressure on the collar only. Our goal is to say "Stay!" less and less until we're saying it only once between "Sit!" and "Take a break!" Conventional training would have us keep him in a Sit-Stay for three full minutes. But this is Wolf Spirit training and this is our best friend. I feel that if we put him in a Sit-Stay and he's held it for a minute or so and we've forgotten about him as we stare into the sunset, then he has every right to lie down and get more comfy—as long as he stays.

Think about it—the "Stay" is our goal here. If we want him stationary any length of time we will use

"Down-Stay," not "Sit." But let him think for himself a little, as long as he is serving the pack well. Repeat this in a cycle for ten minutes and we've completed our first workout.

With a final "Take a break!" he comes over and we praise him like mad. Hold him close. Love him. And you can give him a kernel or two of his dog food at the end of a good workout. *Never give a treat for obeying one command.* This creates a "treat dog" who will want to see a treat before obeying. And the one time that he has to get back to headquarters with THE MESSAGE you won't have a treat. At the end of the workout he has obeyed many commands. You have hunted well together and this is his slice of caribou.

After several workouts you're going to see that you can really count on the stay, so drop the leash after you've said stay. Stay near the leash. Stalk back and forth. If he moves, bark "No!" Take up the leash, give it a snap, get him back in the "Stay," then, repeat "Stay!" and drop the leash. The goal here is to have him in a "Sit-Stay" while you move this way and that around him, not holding the leash while he holds the Stay. You can back up as you say "Stay!"; then, back up further and further. When you're ten, fifteen feet away and he's still holding a good stay then give him "Take a break!" again. He'll run towards you and you'll love and praise him and you've already set in motion off-leash obedience. And you'll use this in your next command.

The next page is a step-by-step summary of the Sit-Stay commands that you can refer to as necessary during the training process.

THE SIT-STAY COMMANDS

Warm-up by practicing "Let's Go! Right Here!"
several times.

1. Position the leash so there is about 3 FEET OF LEASH BETWEEN YOUR LEFT HAND AND BOWSER'S COLLAR.

2. HOLD YOUR LEFT ARM STRAIGHT OUT—KEEPING BOWSER AN ARM'S LENGTH AWAY FROM YOU.

3. Say LET'S GO! softly, letting the dog move a few steps.

4. STOP. As you do so, say Bow-SER! Then, STEP FOR WARD AND THRUST YOUR RIGHT INDEX FINGER TOWARDS HIS EYES, SAYING (in a Stage Whisper) SIT!

5. *IF HE SITS:* Say GOOD BOY! STAY! with a FLAT PALM EXTENDED SHARPLY TOWARDS HIS FACE. Repeat— GOOD BOY! STAY! Then, PRAISE HIM, PET HIM, AND FINISH WITH STAY!

6. *IF HE DOES NOT SIT:* TUG THE LEASH UP AND TOWARDS YOU AT A 45-DEGREE ANGLE UNTIL HE DOES SIT. Then say: STAY!

7. ONCE HE'S IN THE STAY POSITION, move back and forth, saying STAY! If he moves from the sit, say NO!— SNAP!—STAY! *DO NOT REPEAT SIT!*

8. When he has stayed for some time, say TAKE A BREAK! to let him know he's been released, and ENCOURAGE HIM TO COME TO YOU WITH GOOD BOY!

COME-STAY

Several times in this book I've mentioned that what we really want most from our dog is that he come to us when we call him. We want him to be free and happy; to celebrate life with us. And he can be, but only if we have supreme confidence that he will stop whatever he's doing and come directly to us at the precise moment that we call him. To disobey the COME command could be the death of him (or of

> He needs to stop whatever he is doing, come right to us, and sit in front of us.

something he's after). Remember the electrical energy that we are radiating. He's reading it at all moments. So we will praise his good response to this command, we will laugh and love his immediate and eager return to us, but mark this well—you must feel at the core of your being that he WILL come. No compromise, no hesitation, no deviation. We're saving his life here. He will by the grace of God do this or die!

If, as we introduce our dog to the command, COME, he can feel our love and encouragement, our joy at his instant response, and at the same time our grim and unflinching determination that he obey, he will opt for joy and obey. And, for our part, we will never have to see him screaming and rolling over and over as he's processed through the undercarriage of a bus. Did I scare you? Good! Get this right and it won't happen.

When we say "Bow-SER, Come!" he needs to stop whatever he's doing, no matter what it is, and come right to us and sit in front of us. The sit is automatic. We don't tell him to sit, we EXPECT it. And the reason for this is that a favorite wolfie game, and therefore a favorite doggie game, is the body slam. Your dog may make a deal with you in his own mind, "Okay, you've called me and I'm on my way. But when I get there, I'm going to slam into you. Or run right between your legs, or run right around you." He has to know that when we say "Bow-SER, come!" he is to come and sit right in front of us. This will cause him to slow down, become civilized and sit expectantly in front of us. That's very important. So, let's begin. By now you know how a workout goes.

"Are you ready? Good Girl! Let's Go!" Changing directions, enjoying a smooth, well-oiled teamwork, "Right Here!" enjoying the love and bonding, and "Las-SIE! Sit!" "Good Girl! Stay!" And there she is, sitting up perfectly still looking at us as we stand straight up, "Stay" hand out. This is as it's always been and she's expecting "Take a break!" And here's where we introduce the new command.

LASSIE

Holding the leash in our left hand, we move our right hand and arm straight out to the side, level with our shoulder. We lightly tug the leash as we say, "Las-SIE!" and sweep the right hand across to our left knee, bending forward at the waist, and say "Come!" "Good Girl! Right Here!" she should be moving towards us.

COME

Patting our leg with the right hand encourages her. Don't pull her towards you, but do take up the slack in the leash as she approaches. When she's right in front of you, pull up on the leash to get the automatic "Sit" as you say "Good Girl!" You save the final "Good Girl!" for when her butt hits the ground,

RIGHT HERE

GOOD GIRL!

because she hasn't completed the command until she stops whatever she's doing, comes directly to us, and sits right in front of us.

So now we're doing two commands in our workout. And we're also doing both commands in our "blitz" workouts, in our house, and on walks. Remember how we had Bowser hold the Sit-Stay as we dropped the leash and walked away. Well, have him hold that Sit-Stay as we walk away and call him to us—"Bow-ZER, Come!" Because we're not holding the leash now, we'll clap our hands encouragingly in front of us, right where we'd like his head (and therefore the rest of him) to be. When he gets to us, our clapping hands clasp his face in a loving embrace. Our fingers caress behind his ears, slide down to the collar, under his chin, and lifting up towards us we sit him with a loving "Good Boy!"

You can work your dog towards

GOOD BOY!

you if he appears distracted. So many people give up, in panic, if the dog appears hesitant. They assume it's all over, and they run after him saying "Oh God! Help! Bowser! Don't go!" When you do this, you've just made him, the leader. You don't want that. So, stand firm. Say "Hey!" Your voice should be loud, demanding. "Let's Go! Good Boy! (confident) Good Boy!" If that fails, GO GET HIM, and by snap, snap, snapping with the leash, make him know how very important it was that he obey this command.

If he comes to you, but not immediately, you can't correct him physically. However, you can feel disappointment that he didn't come right away. And tell him about it. It's better that you GO GET HIM, correct him, and immediately give him another chance to obey and praise him for his obedience.

Remember the long line in our drills with "Let's Go" and "Right Here"? Well, we're doing the same thing with Bowser with Sit-Stay and Come-Stay. First on the leash in and outside the house. Then with the dropped leash inside the house and a long line outside the house. It's just the same. We're surrounding him with a lot of love and praise for proper response and correction for improper response and we're moving him towards greater and greater freedom as quickly as he can earn it

Again, I am going to summarize the commands step-by-step on the following page so you can easily refer to them during the training process if need be.

THE COME-STAY COMMANDS

1. Begin with the first part of the normal workout (Are You Ready? Good Boy! Let's Go! Right Here! and now adding, Bow-SER? SIT! Good Boy! Stay! Take a Break!). You will want to run through these commands a few times before beginning as sort of a "warm-up" for you and your dog.

2. Put your dog into SIT-STAY, then back up (holding the leash in your left hand), saying: STAY!

3. Bring your RIGHT HAND and ARM UP, STRAIGHT OUT TO THE SIDE OF YOUR BODY AT SHOULDER HEIGHT as you say Bow-SER?

4. Now, say COME! as you BEND FORWARD AT THE WAIST AND SWEEP YOUR RIGHT HAND ACROSS YOUR BODY TO YOUR LEFT KNEE.

5. Say GOOD BOY! (Or Girl). Then, PAT YOUR THIGH, TAKING UP THE SLACK IN THE LEASH AS THE DOG COMES TO YOU. Give a little tug on the leash if necessary. As you take up the slack, the dog has no choice but to be right in front of you. GIVE A LITTLE UPWARD TUG ON THE LEASH AND THE DOG WILL SIT. Save a final GOOD BOY! for the moment when he sits.

6. When the dog seems to have this down, MAKE A TARGET OF YOUR HANDS, CLAPPING THEM ENCOURAGINGLY. When he comes, CARESS HIS FACE AND EARS, THEN SLIDE YOUR FINGERS UNDER HIS COLLAR AND CHIN. PULL UP TO SIT THE DOG. Then say: GOOD BOY!

CHAPTER TWELVE

DOWN-STAY

You now know a lot about dogs in general and about your dog in particular, so I'm not going to repeat the things that it takes to get here. When your dog is good with "Sit" and "Come," it's time to add "Down" to the workouts. You can give him this command after "Sit" or "Come" because in either case he's sitting. Did you know that the Alpha can get a "Down-Stay" from every member of the pack? Oh, yes. And he can get this with little more than a forward step and a meaningful, intent stare. Think about this. Your dog

> Down-Stay is a ritual older than man and has to do with the acceptance of leadership.

views your relationship as a pack relationship. If he won't do a Down-Stay for you, he's not "your" dog, because you're not his Alpha.

Some folks say you should wrestle a dog onto his back and hold him there until he understands and complies with "Down." But, to do this, you must use your hands, and wolves don't have them. "Down-Stay" is a ritual older than man and has to do with the acceptance of leadership based on love, respect, and willingness to follow the one who can best guarantee mutual success. If you followed my advice to this point, all my advice, you are the prime candidate for Alpha in your relationship with your dog. But if your dog resists you on this one, be ready. Never use treats. Never stretch out his paws. This is done by voice and hand signals and pressure to the neck only.

Let me put this in human terms for you. Let's say you know there's a family is moving in across the street, and you step out into your front yard to watch for a moment. Maybe you are going to the curb to check the mail, but you pause for just a moment and take a quick peek at the new neighbors. When they notice you, they knock out a smile and say: *"Hello! We are transcending and superior humans. No harm done this time, because you didn't know. But from now on, whenever one of us look at you, you must bow deeply at the waist. Are we clear on that?"* I know what my response would be, and I can imagine some of your possible responses.

Now your little one most likely was willing to obey "Let's Go!" (that's exciting), "Right Here!" (very rewarding), "Sit! Stay!" (a temporary setback) "Come! Stay!" (that makes "Sit-Stay" enjoyable). However, your puppy just might say: "Bow deeply to you? I don't think so!" Even if he has repeatedly tried to lie down when you've asked him for other things, when you ASK him to lie down on command, he's liable to say "Hell no! That's submissive! And I'm Sparky the Bold! I submit to no one!"

In a pack situation Sparky would at this time receive a sudden and ferocious mauling that would leave him stunned and down, followed by a forward stare that he would never forget. Followed by encouragement. He would say to himself "accept the Alpha's leadership by this ritual or be torn to pieces by the pack—Um . . . let me see here. Join the celebration or die. Actually, now that I think of it, celebrating is a lot better than dying." He has joined the pack.

We will be much more gentle than the wolf, but the implications are all just the same. This is necessary, it serves the pack, it's good for you, and because we love you, you will do this. In an attempt to make this as gentle as possible, we're going to start on our knees in front of little Bowzer. We've taken him through the first part of his workout and he's now sitting eagerly in front of us. We're going to say "Stay!" (using our hand signal as we kneel to keep him in place) and insist that he stay sitting, not moving, as we kneel.

Our hand signal for down is a flat hand, fingers together, as if they were holding a quart of milk, a sort of partially opened fist. We hold this hand signal high over his head (we can snap our fingers to get

him to look up) as we say "Bow-ZER! Dooown!" Draw out the word "down" as we bring the signal down right past his nose, even touching the tip of his nose, and take it down to the ground at his feet. We tap the ground at his feet. He might lie down. If he does, praise him quietly and thank him. He might look down. No matter. If he doesn't lie down at this command, that same hand signal now comes back and rests on his collar where the leash attaches and takes his neck to the ground. His rump may stay in the air for an instant, but he will lie down. Now praise him "Good Boy! This is 'Down'" (use the hand signal) and "Stay!" (using that hand signal). "You Stay! Good Boy!"

Now there's no good reason for a dog to sit from a "Down". You can release him from the Down or call him to you. But for the sake of this training exercise we're going to say "Bow-ZER, Sit!" as we pat our leg, show him the Sit signal and straighten our posture. He should "pop up" into a Sit-Stay. Make sure it's a Sit-Stay. Now, repeat "Bow-ZER! (our hand signal) Down!" as you slip it past his nose, pass it down, then take his neck to the floor. Repeat this over and over giving him the chance to obey before you take his neck to the floor.

You can say "Bow-ZER, Down!" as you give the hand signal down past his nose, to the ground and then hold one foot of leash up to his face, saying "Bow-ZER!" (downward snap). "Bow-ZER" (downward snap), then take his neck to the floor. One of three things will happen: (1) he will obey the hand signal, (2) he will respond to your threat of a snap by obeying your command, or (3) he will win. For God's sake, don't let him win this one. Stay right there and work at it until he does the "Down-Stay" on command.

You'll know what combination of hand signal, threats of snaps, and taking his neck to the ground works for your individual dog as you get into it. Don't get mad! Just do it! Until he obeys! It could take ten minutes or two hours! But if you feel that it's just part of his job and not submission. If you do it because you love him and know that "Down-Stay" is more comfortable than "Sit-Stay" for long periods, then you will both get through this with flying colors and he will learn a priceless lesson. And that is this: *"No matter how hard I fought, she won; she never got mad, she loved me and praised me for this. She is truly Alpha."*

Everything else is easier after your dog learns this. And unlike Sparky the Bold, our best friend isn't missing an ear or any patches of skin. After he's learned the command, of course, you no longer kneel to give him "Down-Stay." The next step is to stand but bend close to him as you give the command and be ready to back the command up with a snap or taking his neck to the floor for disobedience.

Now just do "Down-Stay" as part of the workout—inside, outside, wherever, and whenever. Give him the command while you're just walking along. "Bow-ZER, Down!" and have him do it right now. You can tell him to Sit-Stay, then back up six feet, and say "Bow-ZER Stay!" "Bow-ZER , Stay!" "Bow-ZER, Dooown!" If he tries to come to you, rush in, and say: "No! Down!" He'll get the idea that he must obey these commands right where he is—even if you give them to him from fifty feet.

Another thing you can do is give him the Down-Stay while you're eating. He can be in a Down-Stay right near your chair. (Your foot on the leash at first, of course, will help enforce that.) You can put Ben-Hur on the VCR and have him hold a Down-Stay through the whole thing. If at any time he moves before you have given him "Take a Break!", say "No! (snap) Stay!"

By the way, if you've given him a "Down" and he's holding it as you back away from him (let's say you're now twenty feet away and he's in a Down-Stay), when you give him a "Take a break!" pat your leg and praise him like mad. Let him know, "I'm not punishing you. This is all done out of love and respect, and I really like the way you do it." So you give him "Down! Stay!" and back up thirty feet. Then, "Take a Break! What a Good Boy!" Then you pet him as he comes to you. This is doing two things: it's letting him know that you really appreciate the Down-Stay; it's also enhancing his desire to be someplace else and come towards you when he hears "Take a break!"

Once again, each of these steps is summarized on the following page to guide you through the workout.

THE DOWN-STAY COMMAND

1. Go through all the previous commands, beginning with "Let's Go!" and ending with "Sit-Stay." Your dog is now SITTING IN FRONT OF YOU.

2. KNEEL in front of your dog, USING THE CORRECT HAND SIGNAL FOR STAY AND SAYING STAY! AS YOU KNEEL to make sure he continues his Stay as you kneel.

3. HOLDING THE LEASH IN YOUR LEFT HAND, RAISE YOUR RIGHT HAND OVER HIS HEAD (REFER TO PROPER HAND SIGNAL IN THE FIGURE) as you say Bow-SER!

4. Bring the hand signal DOWN RIGHT PAST HIS NOSE (even brushing his nose) as you say DOOOOWN! and TAP THE FLOOR IN FRONT OF HIS FEET.

5. If He Downs: PRAISE HIM GENTLY BUT LAVISHLY.

6. If He Does *Not* Down: PLACE YOUR RIGHT HAND ON THE LEASH, NEAR HIS COLLAR, AND TAKE HIS NECK TO THE FLOOR. The rest of him will follow!

7. Put him back in a SIT. REPEAT STEPS 3 THROUGH 6 UNTIL HE STAYS DOWN FOR YOU.

8. After giving the DOWN! command and tapping the floor, SHOW HIM THE LEASH IN YOUR HAND and warn him—Bow-SER! SNAP!—THEN TAKE HIS NECK TO THE FLOOR. He will respond to the COMMAND or to the WARNING. It is *ESSENTIAL* that he OBEY this command, so *DO NOT STOP* until you get the Down Command from him.

9. When you DO get the command, PRAISE, CARESS, AND LOVE HIM.

CHAPTER THIRTEEN

HEEL

Heel is a very useful command and it can also be a great deal of fun as we'll see in the next chapter. In "Heel" you and your dog become a motorcycle and side car. He's right there beside you, on your left side. There's an imaginary circle about the size of a basketball that his shoulders are supposed to be in the whole time he's in Heel. The center of that circle is right in line with your left hip, so that if you were to stop walking and stand with your feet together, his right shoulder would be even with your left leg. The idea is that if you walk, he walks; if

> Make this very nice and very slow to start, then pick up the pace and the performance level as you go.

you run, he runs; if you go left or right or walk in a circle, he's right there beside you. When you stop he should automatically sit. You don't tell him to sit. Give him a little upward tug (with the leash) to remind him to sit. When he does sit, say "Good Boy!"

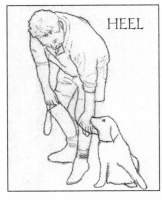

To teach him heel, we put him in a Sit-Stay and then stand, right beside him, his shoulder even with your left leg. Put your right hand in the handle of the leash and gather up a loop of leash that leaves almost no slack when your right hand is held in the center of your stomach. Your right hand is holding the loop, which leaves your left hand free to pat your left leg or tug the leash as needed. You can make this very nice and very slow at first and pick up the pace and the performance level as you go. Bend forward, patting your left leg as you begin to walk, saying "Bow-ZER, Heel! Good Boy! That's it! Heel!" (patting the whole time). "Heel! What a Good Boy!"

Remember, his shoulders are supposed to be in that circle and the leash is to be slack. You're going slowly, patting, saying "Heel! Good Boy! Heel!" And if he falls behind, or gets ahead of, or wanders away from that circle, bring him back into it with a tug (not quite a snap) saying "Heel!" When he's walking along in Heel, praise him "Good Boy! That's it! Heel! What a Good Boy!" (pat, pat)

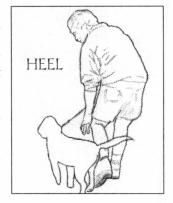

Change directions often, saying "Heel!" at each turn. Then stop. Scuff your feet as you stop at first. As you come to a scuffing stop, pull up on the leash, he should be sitting right beside you. If not, use the warning tone and a tug to sit him. Near the end of your first session, you'll be able to just clear your throat pointedly if he's not sitting and he'll respond.

It's not nice to keep your dog in heel for a whole walk. That's no fun. But, some of the time during each walk, call him to heel, and make a series of turns and stops and starts, giving him lots of praise. Then, finish with "Take a break! Good Boy! Let's Go!"

Two final things, as you're walking along in heel, stop and be serious. Tell him "Stay!" Walk forward a few feet and say "Bow-ZER! Heel!" Pat your calf, "Good Boy!" Keep the leash slack, but tug, if you have to, to get him in the right place and sitting. "Good Boy!" You can also, if you'd like, have him in a Sit-Stay in front of you and say "Bow-ZER! Heel!" Have him either walk to you around your right side and sit at your left in heel, or have him come to your left side and turn around there, sitting at heel. I've never found this necessary in day-to-day work with dogs, but show people like it. "Let's Go!" and "Right Here!" work in most cases, but "Heel!" is very useful in crowded or dangerous situations. So learn it, develop it. I promise you, one day you'll have good use for it.

You'll find the step-by-step instructions for teaching the Heel command on the following page.

THE HEEL COMMAND

Warm-up by doing all of the previous commands.

1.Put the dog in SIT-STAY.

2.STAND beside him so that HIS SHOULDER IS EVEN WITH YOUR LEFT LEG.

3.Put your RIGHT HAND in the handle of the leash, and GATHER UP A LOOP OF LEASH THAT LEAVES ALMOST NO SLACK when your right hand is held at the CENTER OF YOUR STOMACH.

4.BEND FORWARD, PAT YOUR LEFT LEG, and BEGIN TO WALK, saying Bow-SER. HEEL! GOOD BOY! THAT'S IT! HEEL! (patting your leg the whole time). KEEP THE LEASH SLACK.

5.*If he falls behind, gets ahead, or wanders away:* BRING HIM BACK INTO THE CIRCLE WITH A TUG, SAYING HEEL!

6.*When he's walking along in Heel:* PRAISE HIM with GOOD BOY! THAT'S IT! HEEL! WHAT A GOOD BOY.

7.CHANGE DIRECTIONS OFTEN, SAYING HEEL AT EACH TURN. THEN COME TO A SCUFFLING STOP.

8.AS YOU COME TO A STOP, PULL UP ON THE LEASH. He should go into a SIT right beside you.

9.*If he does not SIT:* USE THE WARNING TONE (Bow-SER!) AND A TUG TO SIT HIM.

CHAPTER FOURTEEN

LET'S DANCE—THE PLAYFUL WORKOUT

This is fun. We're now going to put all this stuff we've learned into play. And I do mean play. We're out on our usual walk with Bowser. Bowser has no idea what's coming, but if we do this right he will enjoy this tremendously. We feel mischievous, playful, as we say "Bow-ZER! Are you ready? Are you really ready? Good Boy! Let's Go!" Break away from him. "Let's Go!" Turn again, laugh, "Good Boy!" "Right Here!" Hug him. "Let's Go!" Spin rapidly to face him. "Bowser, sit!" "Good Boy! Stay!" "Bowser, down! Good Boy! Stay! Take a break! Right Here! Good Boy! Bowser, Heel! Turn left and right saying "Heel!" each time. Stop. He sits. "Good Boy!" Now "Heel!" Walk in a circle, pat him, "Heel!" "Good Boy!" Now, "Take a break!"

> The two of you are bonded in a celebration of team work based on love, respect, and desire for mutual success.

The two of you are moving in a series of circles, turns, stops, and starts. He's focused and wagging. You're laughing, but keeping the work sharp, which adds to Bower's enjoyment. You're lightly tugging on the leash After a few of these exercises, you'll see that the leash is absolutely unnecessary. The two of you are bonded in a celebration of teamwork based on love, respect, and desire for mutual success. What did I say at the beginning of this book?

CHAPTER FIFTEEN

PLACE-STAY

Our final command in basic obedience is here at last! You're still giving the blitz workouts, inside and out. Still giving yourself the joy of "Let's Dance!" You no longer need the formal workout. Nice, huh?

If we started at 10 weeks, we're loving our perfectly trained 15-week-old puppy. Well, almost perfectly trained. We're done before most schools recommend you even start. Kind of special, aren't we? "Place" is a

> Place is not a punishment.
> Place is the reward
> for a good workout.

mat Bowser goes to on command. The best "Place" mat is a rubber-backed bath mat because it won't bunch on a smooth floor and is machine washable. "Place" is not a punishment—it's where Bowser goes to be a Good Boy. "Place" is the reward for a good workout. We still don't give treats for a single act of

PLACE-STAY

GOOD BOY –STAY

GOOD BOY

BOWSER PLACE

GOOD BOY –PLACE

obedience. But, if "Place" is the end of his workout, there can be treat on his Place when he gets there. This will cause him to look forward to it eagerly.

To teach Bowser place, we spread the mat out, call him over, pat in the center of it, saying "Good Boy! What a Good Boy!" He should lie down on it. Scratch the place saying "Place!" Scratch his nose, you're bonding him to it. Say "Place! Good Boy!" in a soothing tone. "Place! Good Boy!" and then "Stay!" "Good Boy! Place!" and "Stay!" Now stand up, walk away saying "Stay! Good Boy!" If he tries to leave "No!" Snap! "This is your Place. Stay!" When he's stable, wait a while, and then say "Take a break!" "Good Boy!"

Now, let's say you're eight feet away from Place. Say: "Bowser, Sit!" (or "Down!") "Stay!" You walk to Place so that it is between you and him. Your feet are about three inches from the place. You say, "Bowser, Place!" pointing right at the center of it. "Good Boy! Place!" He should trot right over. As soon as he's got two paws on it say "Good Boy! Stay!" and the Stay hand becomes a caress that stops him right there.

Now, back up as you say "Stay!" He may try to walk around the Place to get to you. You move around the place so that he has to cross it to get to you, and again, as soon as he's got two paws on it you say "Stay!" and caress him as you say "Good Boy!" Have him in a Sit or a Down. Now you're standing between him and the Place. The Place is just a foot or so past you. You say "Bowser, Place!" and your pointing finger sweeps past you and points at the center of the mat. As he gets to you, snap your fingers right over the center of the mat. He has now walked past you and gotten on his place. (Or, he's been tugged past you to the Place if need be.) And you say "Stay!" Step-by-step instructions for teaching Place are at the end of this chapter.

All you have to do now is slowly increase the distance that you're standing from the Place until you can send him to the Place from any distance. It's important to know that you can use this command right away. If your doorbell rings two minutes after this lesson you can call him to Place before opening the door. Make this the last command in a workout. Send him to Place to get his slice of caribou, or kernel of dog food or biscuit.

What are some uses for place? Let's say that you and Bowser are going to take a drive in the country, and you know you're going to let him out to romp around for a while. Now he gets his feet muddy. Well, clever you, you've thought to bring the Place. So now, when he gets back in the car, his muddy feet are on the Place, not on the upholstery of your car. Let's say company comes over. Before you open the door, you say: "Bowser, Place!" And you wait until he's bored with the company, then give him "Take a break!" Then, he'll walk over and say hello and there won't be a big fuss. While you're eating dinner, you can use this command to keep him away from the table and avoid the issue of begging for people food. So you say: "Bowser, Place!" "What a Good Boy! Stay!" Off he goes to his Place, and you finish your dinner in peace and without those guilty feelings.

Let's say you're running around the house trying to get things done and you realize this is the third time you've tripped over Bowser. Don't get mad. Turn this into a win-win. Say "I know Bowser. Let's get on your Place!" And you walk over there and point to the Place, "What a Good Boy!" and then "Stay!" Now he's happily on his Place and you're not tripping over him. You've turned this possibly negative thing into something positive. Keep in mind Place is not punishment—it's Bowser's spot to go to knowing he's a Good Boy.

Okay. That's it! You've properly selected your puppy, brought him home, modified his behavior, taken him through a course of obedience that's led him to be eager and happy, and now you're done.

All we have to do now is incorporate the attitudes—and the discipline—that we've learned in behavior modification and regularly schedule the quick blitz workouts into our lives. This will keep the relationship with your dog fresh and happy. It will keep the obedience current and sharp. And it will always reinforce the loving bond that is now formed between you. Enjoy your well-trained puppy. May you both live long, healthy, and joyous lives.

PLACE

For this exercise, you will need to have a mat, rug, etc. that you will designate as "Place."

1. SPREAD OUT THE MAT, CALL THE DOG OVER, AND PAT THE CENTER OF THE MAT Saying: GOOD BOY! WHAT A GOOD BOY! (The dog should come to the mat and lie down on it.)

2. SCRATCH the Mat, saying PLACE!, then SCRATCH HIS NOSE and say PLACE! GOOD BOY! USING a SOOTHING TONE.

3. Say STAY! GOOD BOY! PLACE! STAY!

4. STAND UP and WALK AWAY saying STAY! GOOD BOY!

5. If he tries to leave: Say NO!—Snap!— THIS IS YOUR PLACE. STAY!

6. When he's stable, WAIT A WHILE, then say TAKE A BREAK! GOOD BOY!

7. STARTING ABOUT 8 FEET AWAY FROM PLACE, SAY: Bow-SER, SIT! STAY! Walk to the PLACE so that it is BETWEEN YOU AND HIM. POINT to the CENTER of the PLACE Saying GOOD BOY! PLACE! and he should go right over to it. When he has TWO PAWS on it, say GOOD BOY! STAY! (WAIT A WHILE, THEN SAY, TAKE A BREAK! GOOD BOY!)

8. SIT HIM and STAND BETWEEN Him and the PLACE. Say Bow-SER, SWEEPING YOUR POINTING FINGER ACROSS YOU and POINT at the CENTER of the Mat. As he gets to you SNAP Your Fingers over the CENTER of PLACE. When he is ON PLACE, say STAY. GOOD BOY!

ROVIN'

(best read with an Irish accent in mind)

I like roomy trousers, I do
Of corduroy, in gray or blue
And welly boots with thick wool socks
They're very good amongst the rocks
And the shaggy dog that by me sits
And waits for me to grab my stick
And the walkin' hat that nicely fits
For then it's down to the sea we'll go
Where the wind and water wildly blow
And he'll help me be the child I was
That walked here long ago.

Printed in the United States
201446BV00003B/1-51/A

9 780966 888454